Lizards

Lizards

by Claudia Schnieper/photographs by Max Meier

A Carolrhoda Nature Watch Book

Carolrhoda Books, Inc./Minneapolis

Thanks to James E. Gerholdt, The Remarkable Reptiles,
for his assistance with this book.

This edition first published 1990 by Carolrhoda Books, Inc.
Copyright © 1988 by Kinderbuchverlag Luzern.
Original edition published 1988 by Kinderbuchverlag Luzern
Lucern, Switzerland, under the title EIDECHSEN. Adapted by
Carolrhoda Books, Inc.
All additional material supplied for this edition © 1990 by
Carolrhoda Books, Inc.

LIBRARY OF CONGRESS CATALOGING-IN-PUBLICATION DATA

Schnieper, Claudia.
 [Eidechsen. English]
 Lizards / by Claudia Schnieper : photographs by Max Meier.
  p.   cm.
 Translation of: Eidechsen.
 "A Carolrhoda nature watch book."
 Summary: Discusses the physiology and behavior of lizards
generally and presents some detail about specific species.
  ISBN 0-87614-405-9 (lib. bdg.)
  1. Lizards—Juvenile literature. [1. Lizards.] I. Meier, Max,
ill. II. Title.
QL666.L2S36513   1990
597.95—dc20   89-22158
                                                       CIP
                                                        AC

Manufactured in the United States of America

1 2 3 4 5 6 7 8 9 10 99 98 97 96 95 94 93 92 91 90

Whether you are walking through a meadow, searching for life in a seemingly lifeless desert, hiking through the woods, or even skiing down a trail, there is one kind of animal you might find—the lizard. Lizards belong to a class of animal called reptiles. Turtles and tortoises, worm lizards, snakes, tuataras, and crocodilians are also included in this class. Of all these reptiles, lizards are the most adaptable. They are able to live in most every kind of environment and are found on every continent in the world except Antarctica. One kind of lizard even lives in the cold climate above the Arctic Circle.

Reptiles have existed for about 300 million years. They are thought to be the first animals that were able to live completely on land. Animals that existed before the reptiles had to spend at least part of their lives in water. For 120 million years, reptiles ruled the animal kingdom. Their rise to dominance was, at least in part, due to their success in adapting to many different kinds of environments. Then, 80 million years ago, the reptile's reign came to an end. No one knows exactly what happened, but most everyone agrees that whatever killed most of the lizards and all of the dinosaurs must have been the result of a major event in the earth's history.

Notice the wet, mucous skin of this amphibian, the spotted salamander (Salamandra salamandra).

One of the first problems that reptiles had to face millions of years ago, when they came out of the water and began to spend more time on land, was how to keep their bodies from drying out. The solution was to be found in their skin. Amphibians, the reptiles' ancestors, faced a similar problem. They adapted by developing the ability to produce a wet, mucous coating for their skin. This coating kept their bodies from drying out, but amphibians still needed to spend part of their daily lives in the water. Reptiles adapted differently.

7

Lacerta lepida, *the eyed lizard, measures about 26 inches (65 cm) from its snout to the tip of its tail.*

For all animals, skin acts as a barrier between other deeper tissues and the environment. Lizards, as well as other animals, have two major layers of skin, the **epidermis** and the **dermis.** The epidermis is the outer layer of skin. In lizards, it is made of **keratin,** which thickens and forms scales.

Scales can be a variety of shapes and sizes. Some scales are smooth, and some scales have a keel, or ridge, down the center; some scales overlap, and some line up against one another. The varia-tion in the scale patterns throughout a lizard's body and head help us identify each **species,** or type, of lizard. Look closely at the eyed lizard in this picture. Its body is covered with different kinds of scales arranged in a variety of pat-terns. Keeled scales have formed on its tail. Its belly is covered by large, rec-tangular scales, while the back of this lizard is covered with teardrop-shaped scales. The scales on top of its head are irregularly shaped and flat.

Lizards' skins do not grow with the rest of their bodies. Whenever lizards grow too big for their skin, the outer keratin layer is shed. Before shedding their old skin, lizards become listless and eat less than usual. Most lizards shed their old skin in bits and pieces, unlike snakes, who usually shed their skins in one continuous strip. New skin is brighter and looser, giving lizards room in which to grow. During the first two to four years of their lives, lizards grow quickly, so they shed more often than they do as adults. But lizards never stop growing, so they shed their skin periodically throughout their entire lives.

This sand lizard (Lacerta agilis) *is in the process of shedding its skin.*

Two male mountain chameleons (Chamaeleo montium) *are fighting. The lighter colored chameleon is winning the fight. Notice how the weaker chameleon becomes darker as he realizes that he's losing the fight.*

The inner layer of skin, the dermis, is not shed. It's made up of tissues, blood vessels, and nerves. Most of the lizard's **pigment cells** are found in the dermis as well. The pigment cells determine a lizard's color. Most of the pigment cells contain **melanin,** a brown or black pigment. Other pigment cells may be yellow, white, or red. The amount and placement of melanin layered under the other colored pigment cells determine a lizard's colors.

Some lizards change their colors in response to their moods. Chameleons are the most dramatic example. When fighting, their color changes, depending on whether they are winning or losing. Their moods trigger a response from the lizards' **glands.** Lizards' colors also change when they're mating and in response to temperature.

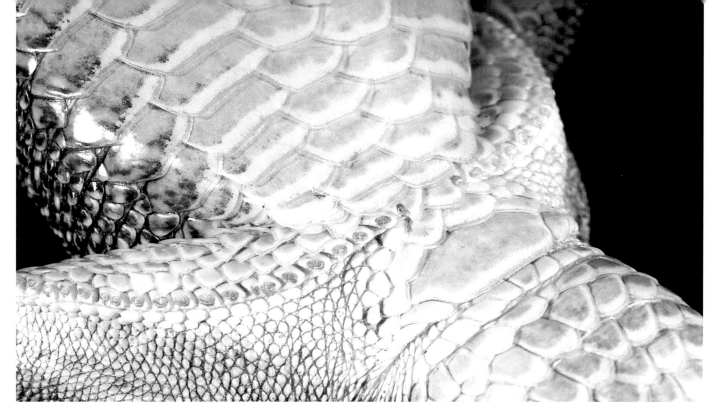

You can clearly see pores on the thighs of this emerald lizard (Lacerta viridis).

All animals have glands. Glands are specialized cells that remove certain material from blood, then secrete the material from the body through pores. We have pores all over our bodies. When we get hot, we secrete liquid through our pores to cool our bodies. In other words, we sweat. Lizards have pores only on their thighs and at the base of their tails. Since lizards do not have pores all over their bodies, they don't sweat the way we do. Liquid, therefore, is not lost through their skin—another adaptation to prevent water loss from their bodies.

Sweating is an example of glandular secretion, but lizards do not sweat. Instead glandular secretions help lizards recognize others of their own species. In particular, these secretions help males and females of a species recognize each other so they can mate successfully. Young male lizards often wander as far as 300 feet (91.5 m) in search of a free territory. Male lizards mark their territories by secreting a waxlike substance. Once they've claimed a territory, male lizards begin courting.

The mating pair of sand lizards (left) and of emerald lizards (above) found each other by means of glandular secretions. Notice the difference in colors between the males and females.

Courtship of the emerald lizard

From courtship to birth, the process of reproduction varies for different species of lizard. The courtship ritual is important to the lizard's success in finding a mate. When a male lizard is in a courting mood, his skin becomes brighter and more colorful. The emerald lizard pictured here has found a potential mate. He courts her by walking toward her using jerky movements. He circles the female to show off his brilliant blue throat. Only a female emerald lizard will respond favorably to this male's courtship. If she is not an emerald lizard, or if she is not ready to mate, she will run away. Even if she is interested in mating, she is torn between fleeing from the male lizard and allowing him to mate with her. She reacts to this conflict by **treading**—she presses her body to the ground, bobs her head, and moves her legs up and down.

Still treading, the female moves forward, and the male grabs her tail. Either the female pulls the male behind her, or the male pushes the female forward. This activity may last for as long as one hour. The male then bites the female on the flank and pulls himself on top of her.

Now that it is time to mate, the male's reproductive organ is pushed out of his body through his cloacal opening. The **cloaca** (kloh-AY-ka) is an opening that is found in both male and female lizards. It is used for the elimination of wastes and for reproduction. To mate, the male lizard inserts his reproductive organ into the female's cloaca. He deposits his **sperm,** or male reproductive cells, into the female's body. After the lizards have mated, they go their separate ways.

Three weeks after mating, the female emerald lizard is visibly heavier because the eggs inside her body are developing. She cannot move as quickly as she used to—she is sluggish and eats very little. Before mating, she was active during the day. Now, because she cannot protect herself very well against predators, she moves about at night, searching for the perfect place to lay her eggs.

Unlike most other lizards, young emerald lizards band together in groups during their first year.

Lizards usually lay eggs in sand or under rocks. The pregnant emerald lizard (pictured at left) uses her feet to tunnel 12 inches (30 cm) into the sand. At the end of the tunnel, she digs out a little cave. Emerald lizards lay between 5 and 22 eggs that are ½ inch (1.5 cm) long and ⅓ inch (1 cm) wide. After she lays her eggs, the female lizard covers them with dirt. She has now finished her "motherly" duties and goes on her way. Damp sand is an ideal place for a lizard to lay her eggs because it absorbs and retains heat. The warmth of the sun, not the female's body, hatches the eggs.

As soon as the young lizards hatch, they look for food. A typical meal is insects, snails, or tiny spiders.

During their first year of life, young emerald lizards band together in groups. When faced with danger, the lizards run in different directions, then stop and remain motionless. This confuses their enemies and increases each lizard's chance of survival.

This sand lizard uses the same methods that the emerald lizard uses to lay her eggs. Although lizards' eggs are somewhat protected in the soil, they may not all hatch. Some of the eggs may be eaten by other animals or attacked by bacteria and fungi.

After 4 to 12 weeks, those sand lizard eggs that have not been destroyed have doubled in size. The **embryo**, or developing baby lizard, is growing inside the egg. It is protected by **albumen** (al-BYU-muhn), or egg white. Attached to the embryo is the egg yolk, which is the embryo's food source. With its back to the shell and its belly toward the yolk, the tiny lizard embryo grows until it is developed enough to live on its own.

Shortly before hatching, the eggs become spotted and shriveled. When the baby sand lizard is ready to hatch, it tears at the shell with its tiny **egg tooth.** With much effort, the hatching lizard pushes its head out of the egg, then rests in this position for many hours. After it has rested, the lizard crawls out of the egg completely. The egg tooth drops off shortly after the lizard hatches. The newly hatched sand lizard pictured on the next page is still attached to its yolk sac. This does not usually happen.

Not all species of lizard lay eggs. Those that do, lay eggs with thick shells that were first developed in some reptiles to protect the eggs from drying out. This shelled egg is another adaptation that helped lizards come out of the water and live on land.

Lacerta vivipara

The Viviparous (vy-VIHP-uhr-uhs) lizard, one of the most adaptable of all the lizards, is able either to lay eggs or give birth to live young, depending on the region in which it lives. The Viviparous lizard may be found as far south as Italy and as far north as the northern tip of Europe, above the Arctic Circle. No other reptile is able to live so far into the cold regions of the world. During the coldest times of the year, the Viviparous lizard finds a protected place in the ground and enters a sleeplike state called **hibernation**. The lizard's heartbeat and breathing slow down, and its body temperature falls. By hibernating, the Viviparous lizard can survive the cold temperatures.

Pictured above is a pregnant Viviparous lizard shortly before the birth of her young. Notice how thick she is around the middle. She may have as many as 10 eggs developing inside her. The length of time that they will remain in her body, and the stage of development that her young will reach by the time of birth depend on the climate.

21

In regions where the climate is warm, eggs are carried for a short period of time. When these eggs are laid, the embryos may not be fully developed, so the eggs are laid in a hole and covered with sand or dirt. The young continue to develop for a few more days, then they hatch and crawl out of the hole.

In regions where the climate is cold, the young may hatch while they are still in their mother's body. The climate in these northern regions is so harsh that eggs laid in the ground would not develop and would probably freeze. So the Viviparous lizard has adapted by carrying her eggs inside her body. She is a walking incubator—as the mother is warmed by the sun, so are her eggs.

While in their mother's body, the Viviparous lizard embryos grow in a parchmentlike egg covering until they are developed enough to live on their own. They do not get their food from their mother through an umbilical cord like mammals do, but from the egg yolk, like other lizards. Here you can see a female Viviparous lizard giving birth.

In this case, the young are born while they are still within the parchmentlike egg covering. Immediately, these newborn lizards free themselves from the egg. Some of the young are still attached to the yolk sac. The newborn Viviparous lizard is about 1¾ inches (4.5 cm) long.

Ruin lizards (Podarcis sicula) *live mainly in Italy and Yugoslavia. Their tails are almost three times longer than their bodies.*

Most adult lizards do not care for their eggs or their young. The female ruin lizard, however, does care for her eggs for a short time. She lays her eggs in a hole—usually under large stones—pushes dirt over them, and presses the surface down with her snout. During the next two to three days, she often checks her nest and chases intruders away.

Some lizards reproduce only at certain times of the year, while others reproduce throughout the year. Environmental factors, such as temperature, humidity, rainfall, food availability, and amount of daylight, determine the frequency of reproduction.

Above: *A sand lizard absorbs warmth from a piece of corrugated iron.*

Lizards and other reptiles are greatly affected by environmental factors in other ways as well—they are **ectotherms** (EK-toh-therms). Some people call ectotherms cold-blooded animals because they cannot produce heat for themselves. But their blood isn't really cold, so scientists prefer to call reptiles ectotherms. Ectotherms depend on the warmth of the sun and the coolness of the shade to maintain their body temperature. **Endotherms** maintain their body temperature internally. Because this requires much energy, endotherms need to eat more than ectotherms. Since they eat relatively small amounts of food, ectotherms like lizards are able to live in areas where food is scarce, increasing their ability to adapt to different environments.

Above: *A sand lizard comes out of its sleeping place in the rocks to bask in the sun.*
Left: *Wall lizards* (Podarcis muralis) *are often seen on walls of houses. They are welcome visitors because they eat insects and spiders, and they may become quite friendly.*

Early in the morning, lizards come out of their sleeping places. Since they cannot regulate their body temperature internally, lizards depend on the sun and the shade to keep their bodies at an ideal temperature. In order to do this, lizards bask in the sun to warm themselves. When they become too warm, they move to the shade to cool down. They may also change position so that more or less of their bodies are exposed to the direct rays of the sun. They also absorb warmth from the surfaces on which they bask.

Above: *The dark-colored milos lizard* (Podarcis milensis) *in the top picture is able to absorb heat faster than the light-colored Adriatic wall lizard* (Podarcis melisselensis) *in the bottom picture.*

Right: *Latastia longicaudata revoili*

Another way lizards regulate their body temperature is with their glands. Early in the day, or when the temperature is cool, their glands secrete a substance that spreads melanin in their skin. This makes the lizard's skin darker. Dark-colored skin is better able to absorb

the sun's warmth than light-colored skin, so lizards with dark-colored skin can warm up more rapidly.

When lizards bask in the sun, they are sitting targets for their enemies. Sometimes their enemies are other lizards. Fighting between male lizards may become quite violent, as we can see in this picture of three African collard lizards. While two lizards are mating, they are attacked by a third, male lizard. The two males fight, while the female gets tossed around violently.

A Balkan racer (Coluber gemonensis) *devours an emerald lizard.*

After losing part of its tail, this common gecko (Tarentola mauritanica) *has developed a forked tail.*

Lizards also have to defend themselves against other enemies. Animals such as snakes, hawks, and cats eat lizards. Because lizards could not normally win a fight against these predators, lizards have developed an unusual way of defending themselves—they can drop their tails.

A lizard's tail contains many bones, called **vertebrae** (VER-tuh-bray). Each vertebra has a special area of weakness in its center. If an enemy grabs a lizard's tail, the vertebra will separate at its point of weakness. All the tissues and blood vessels at that point separate as well. The muscles in the separated tail contract, causing the tail to twitch and flail around. This activity attracts the predator's attention long enough for the lizard to run away. Not only can lizards lose their tails to distract predators, but they can also grow new tails. New tails grow back within a few months. They are usually shorter, thicker, and paler in color than the original tails.

This wall lizard has grown a new tail. The breaking point is clearly visible.

Lizards are predators too. They use their eyes and ears to hunt mainly insects and spiders. Because their environments are so varied, lizards eat many different creatures. Lizards in southern regions may eat snails, caterpillars, birds' eggs, small snakes, young mice, and even blossoms, berries, and grapes. Other tasty meals for lizards might include bees, hornets, and even young lizards. The Adriatic wall lizard (pictured on page 28) eats mainly vegetation but has developed a relationship with seagulls that both lizards and seagulls benefit from. Adriatic wall lizards eat the seagulls' droppings, and in so doing, they keep the rocks clean. Because the rocks are clean, parasites, which could have infected the seagulls, don't develop.

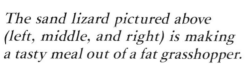

The sand lizard pictured above (left, middle, and right) is making a tasty meal out of a fat grasshopper.

Below right: *The Canary Island lizard* (Lacerta galloti) *eats mostly fruit, seeds, vegetation, and the droppings of goats and rabbits.*

A transparent lower eyelid is protecting the eye of this emerald lizard. You can also see the ear opening on the side of its head.

When a bird of prey circles in the sky, lizards run for cover. When an insect flies overhead, lizards seize it for their dinner. Their sharp eyesight, which responds primarily to movement, helps lizards tell the difference between enemy and dinner. Most lizards have upper eyelids that they can open and close, and lower eyelids that are transparent. Even when the transparent lids are closed, lizards can see through them. Lids protect lizards' eyes from thorns, burrs, and dirt. Besides movement, lizards also see colors.

Lizards have a good sense of hearing too. The eardrum, which transmits sounds to the inner ear, can be clearly seen under a lizard's temple. Lizards can hear low tones better than high tones, and what they can't hear, they can feel. Lizards are able to feel the slightest vibrations in the ground.

This emerald lizard is using its tongue to lap up water from a creek.

The entrances to the Jacobson's organ are clearly visible on the roof of the mouth of this sand lizard.

Lizards use their tongues as additional sense organs. They flick their tongues in and out of their mouths, picking up tiny particles from their environment. Their tongues push the particles into their **Jacobson's organs.** In lizards, the Jacobson's organ is a pair of tiny pockets lined with sensory cells, which are located at the roof of the mouth near the lizard's nose. The sensory cells examine and "translate" the particles for the brain, providing it with information about the lizard's environment. For example, a male lizard darts his tongue at a spot that has been marked by another male lizard. As soon as his tongue scrapes the molecules against his Jacobson's organ, the report is passed to his brain that he is in another lizard's territory. This process takes only seconds. Lizards with long, forked tongues have Jacobson's organs that are more developed than the Jacobson's organs of lizards with short, broad tongues. And those with long, forked tongues flick them more frequently.

Other animals have Jacobson's organs. The animal we most associate with this organ, and with tongue flicking, is the snake. The animal pictured here is not a snake, though, it's a legless lizard.

Legless lizards have been developing for millions of years. Over time, the number of their vertebrae increased, so their bodies became longer than the average lizard's. At the same time, legless lizards became more slender than other lizards, and their legs became useless. Legless lizards and snakes aren't really missing legs, they've just developed into the best possible form for their survival. These changes have helped them adapt to their environments. Legless lizards tend to live on the ground and burrow in the soil.

The slowworm (Anguis fragilis) *is a legless lizard. Its forked tongue is clearly visible.*

One kind of legless lizard is the slowworm. Pictured below is a slowworm that has just given birth to eight young. They were born in a filmy egg skin that is 10 times thinner than the egg skin of the Viviparous lizard. The young wriggle out of the egg skin and immediately venture out on their own. The slowworm, like the Viviparous lizard, gives birth to live young.

Like other lizards, legless lizards like this slowworm can drop their tails to distract their enemies. Unlike snakes, legless lizards shed their skins in bits and pieces.

Slowworms may be found in European gardens, marshes, and forests and can reach a length of 1½ feet (50 cm). They hunt in the early morning and late afternoon, searching for slugs and earthworms. Their curved teeth are pointed backward, an adaptation that helps them catch their slippery prey. Slowworms are harmless and useful lizards. Farmers recognize them as natural predators responsible for controlling pests. But people are the slowworm's worst enemies because they fear its snakelike form. When caught by a person, or attacked by another enemy, slowworms drop their tails just like any other lizard would. But because the slowworm's tail is one-half to two-thirds of its body, it seems as though the slowworm's body has broken in half.

The sheltopusik, or alligator worm, is another kind of legless lizard. But this lizard has two little wart-shaped leg stumps on either side of its cloacal opening—a reminder that its ancestors had legs. The sheltopusik is one of the largest lizards, measuring about 4¾ feet (1.45 m) in length. It lives along the coast of Italy and in parts of Asia. Snails are its favorite food. Sheltopusiks eat the shells as well as the snails, then they rub their snouts along the ground to wipe the snails' slime off their faces.

Ophisaurus apodus

Lizards are living examples of how species can adapt over time to their changing environments. The variety of lizards along with their ancient heritage allows us to see adaptations in the making. The development of scales, the special way lizards regulate their body temperature, their ability to change color, their reproductive methods, their variety of shapes and sizes, and their special defenses are all ways that lizards have developed to live in their changing world.

But many lizards are threatened with **extinction.** If we are not careful, whole species of lizards may die. One way we can help lizards is by getting our communities together to preserve abandoned gravel pits, hedges, meadows, ponds, and marshlands for reptiles to live in. With a little consideration and a little work, these animals may live for at least another million years.

GLOSSARY

albumen: the white of an egg that forms a protective layer of fluid around a developing lizard embryo

cloaca: an opening in reptiles used for reproduction and waste elimination

dermis: the inner layer of skin that is made up of tissues, blood vessels, and nerves

ectotherms: animals whose body temperatures are controlled by their environment. Another word used to describe this condition is *cold-blooded.*

egg tooth: a special tooth that many young reptiles use to cut through their egg shells. After the reptile hatches, the egg tooth falls off.

embryo: an animal in the early stage of development, before birth or hatching

endotherms: animals whose temperatures are controlled by their internal body systems. Another word used to describe this condition is *warm-blooded.*

epidermis: the outer layer of skin

extinction: the occurance of all members of a species dying out

glands: specialized cells that remove specific material from blood, then secrete the material from the body

hibernation: passing the winter in a sleeplike state. An animal's breathing and heartbeat slow down, and its body temperature drops.

Jacobson's organ: a special organ on the roof of a lizard's mouth that combines the senses of smell and taste

keratin: the material that makes up the horny outer layer of a reptile's skin

melanin: a pigment that produces black or brown colors in animals or plants

pigment: materials in the cells of animals and plants that produce different colors

species: a group of animals or plants that share similar characteristics and can interbreed

sperm: an animal's male reproductive cells

treading: an activity performed by a female lizard when she is torn between running away from or mating with a male lizard

vertebrae: the bony segments that make up the spine

INDEX

ABOUT THE AUTHOR

Claudia Schnieper began her career as a book seller and is now a free-lance writer, editor, and translator. She is the author of several nature books for children, including the Carolrhoda Nature Watch books *Chameleons* and *Amazing Spiders*. Ms. Schnieper lives in an old farmhouse near Lucerne, Switzerland, with her husband, Robert, various cats and dogs, and a parrot.

ABOUT THE PHOTOGRAPHER

Max Meier is a free-lance photographer who specializes in photographing animals. When he is not busy taking pictures of spiders, frogs, and lizards, he works in the Veterinary Hospital in Zurich, Switzerland. Mr. Meier has photographed several nature books for children and an adult book on amphibians and reptiles. He makes his home in Zurich.